Morocco

DESIGN | DECOR

Translated by **Monica Sandor**
English language edition project managed by **Johanna Gruber**
Created in collaboration with **Carole Hardoüin**

British Library Cataloguing-in-Publication Data
A catalogue record for this book is available from the British Library.

ISBN-13: 978-1-58479-587-5
ISBN-10: 1-58479-587-5

Printed and bound in Spain
10 9 8 7 6 5 4 3 2 1

HNA
harry n. abrams, inc.
a subsidiary of La Martinière Groupe

Morocco

Philippe Saharoff & Francesca Torre

D E S I G N | D E C O R

Stewart, Tabori & Chang
New York

Foreword

For many centuries, the many cultural and commercial ties between Spain and the western Maghreb have inspired a highly refined art of living in these regions. The sumptuous decor of certain residences, far surpassing our own notions of comfort, has held great fascination for European writers and artists who went to Morocco in search of inspiration. This extraordinary attraction, so aptly described by the French painter Eugene Delacroix, can be said to have served as the impetus for the great nineteenth-century enthusiasm for orientalist art. Since that time, the strong power of seduction exerted by this country has never flagged. This is obvious to anyone who takes a stroll through the heart of the imperial Moroccan cities and steps into one of the *riads*. Once past the heavy, studded doors, you find yourself inside a sheltered world with its marvelously rich interiors, where a centuries-old way of life endures.

Beyond the customary zigzag entrance that safeguards the privacy of the occupants, you step into an inner courtyard ringed by exuberant trees. The captivating aromas of orange, jasmin, jacaranda, and date palm trees mingle with the scent of rosebushes. Far from the bustle of the street, the perpetual murmur of a fountain or basin serves as the backdrop to the serene atmosphere of this little garden of Eden. It is worth recalling that *riad* means "garden" and by extension represents the earthly paradise. The various private rooms on the ground floor and upper stories are arranged around this open-air central court.

Let us guide you from room to room through these opulent interiors, where life is good. The tour will be punctuated by advice, tips, and addresses to help you design and decorate your own home in the spirit of Morocco.

The Living Space

With its many salons, the Moroccan *riad* was conceived first and foremost to serve as a vast reception area. A large part of social life unfolds in these spaces. Guests are received in small open-air salons, under the arcades, or on the galleries of the patio, or else in a living room of majestic dimensions.

Women in particular devote a great deal of attention to decorating this room, which is devoted entirely to entertaining—an age-old Moroccan tradition.

In the afternoon, serving mint tea becomes a veritable ceremony. "Gazelle horns" (crescent-shaped pastries filled with almond paste and coated with sugar), gypsum flowers, and a thousand and one delicacies filled with dried fruits, dates, and nuts are offered along with the tea, which is poured with a broad gesture in order to release its aroma. This is generally a task reserved for the head of the house. The rules of hospitality dictate that he offer his guests three infusions of mint tea, made up of loose green tea, fresh peppermint, and a copious amount of sugar. Seated on a voluptuous bench filled with an abundance of cushions in warm, bright colors, the participants can savor this moment of relaxation. Etiquette demands that one withdraw after the third glass.

In the evening the atmosphere becomes more refined, under the sparse light of the flickering lamps and lanterns. Meals are eaten at a low table set between the divans and the poufs. The master of the house says the appropriate phrase, the *Bismillah*, which means "in the name of God," marking the start of the meal. On platters made of chiseled brass, a succession of delicate dishes are brought forth in a clearly defined order.

SCULPTED CEILINGS

Formerly abundant in the Atlas Mountain massifs, cedar lies at the origin of an ancient woodworking tradition. It has been used for a very long time in traditional construction, furniture making, and decorative arts. In the narrow passageways of the souks, the heady fragrance of cedar signals the presence of cabinetmakers and carpenters who practice an art that has been passed on from generation to generation. These artisans design shelves, low tables, jewelry boxes, and finely-chiseled chests of cedarwood from the Middle Atlas range. Its pale color and deliciously peppery scent make it a frequent choice in all Moroccan homes. Rotproof when completely dry, this softwood requires no treatment and is well suited for carving, sculpting, and painting. On the finely carved ceilings, cedar lends itself both to sculpting in bas-relief and to inlaying with geometrical motifs such as lozenges and star-shaped polygons which, along with highly stylized floral patterns, are used to create scrolls also known as arabesques. To enliven the space and compensate for the lack of natural light in certain rooms, these ceilings are sometimes adorned with vivid colors. The paint accentuates the reliefs formed by sculpting the wood. Ceilings with a cupola are in turn decorated by muqarnas, little wooden stalac-tites forming honeycomb patterns that attest to the virtuosity of the craft.

1 The carved and painted cedar ceilings attest to the virtuosity of this craft.

2 and 3 Spectacular vaulted ceilings are sometimes made of raw bricks, an ancient skill revived by certain Moroccan architects.

4 The painted decor of the interior shutters complements the carefully designed wall.

3

ARABESQUES

You may want to use ready-made stencils to decorate your ceiling with arabesques. Or you could make your own stencils using motifs you may have found on a carpet or a piece of pottery. Cut the motif out of a piece of thick cardboard or a sheet of acetate. This way, you can personalize your decor, making it more original.

If you choose the stencilling technique, use a single-coat acrylic paint for the ceiling that can be applied without dripping. Odorless and easy to clean in the case of smudging, this type of paint also has the advantage of drying rapidly. Aerosol paint dries immediately and can produce good results, but make sure to try it out on a small surface first.

SCULPTED DOORS

In the inextricable labyrinth of the medinas' alleyways, heavy sculpted doors protect the intimacy of the *riads*. The sole exterior decorative element, these monumental doors are made up of two panels and can reach a height of four to five meters. Their generous proportions point to the presence of rich palaces and opulent dwellings. Mounted on two pivots from within, they open sideways to separate the rooms from the patios. Cut into these majestic portals, two little doors, on a more human scale, allow the occupants to enter. In the twinkling of an eye you can move between the street and the patio, from the public square into private space, out of the effervescence into silence. The doors open onto a garden planted with orange trees and sweet-smelling plants, where the crystal-clear waters of a fountain flow quietly, bestowing a welcome freshness on the enclosure.

These magnificent doors, adorned with large studs and inlaid motifs, may also be topped with a substantial canopy in sculpted plaster, covered with green tiles. These are characterized by a hierarchy of several levels, created by low relief decorations on wood and plaster. Other elements of the Islamic decorative repertoire, such as Arabic calligraphy, sometimes contribute to enriching the fine handiwork. Protective symbols such as stars and the hand of Fatima (symbols of fertility, prosperity and good fortune) are placed on the doors to ward off evil spirits.

1 Door inlaid with star polygons in mother-of-pearl, topped with chiseled plaster.

2 A small door cut into the studded portal allows the occupants access.

3 A marked taste for abundant decoration is evident from this superb ceiling in painted wood.

PAINTED WOOD

Zouak, or painting on wood, is a highly regarded craft within Moroccan architecture and decoration. Its lively and bright tones—green, yellow, red and blue—cover ceilings, inside shutters, window frames, and mirrors as well as furniture. Some of the paints are made with an egg-yolk base, especially those intended for decorating ocher backgrounds. In former times the surface to be painted was systematically covered with a basecoat of red paint. Even today the paintbrushes are still made by the artisans themselves out of pieces of cedarwood and hair from a donkey's tail.

To obtain a wooden surface that is quick and easy to paint, it is best to remove the previous layers of paint with a chemical stripper. If the wood is new, a liquid sealer should be used in order to make it easier to apply the color. While microporous paint made of glycerol resin that is specially intended for wood does not require any undercoat, as it is waterproof and antifungal, it is less durable than traditional paints.

To lend an oriental note to your doors or furniture, stenciling can once again offer a broad range of decorative ideas. This process, both inexpensive and easy, can achieve great effect with a small quantity of paint. It is best to use repositionable glue to ensure that the stencil adheres perfectly to the surface, to prevent the paint from seeping under the edges.

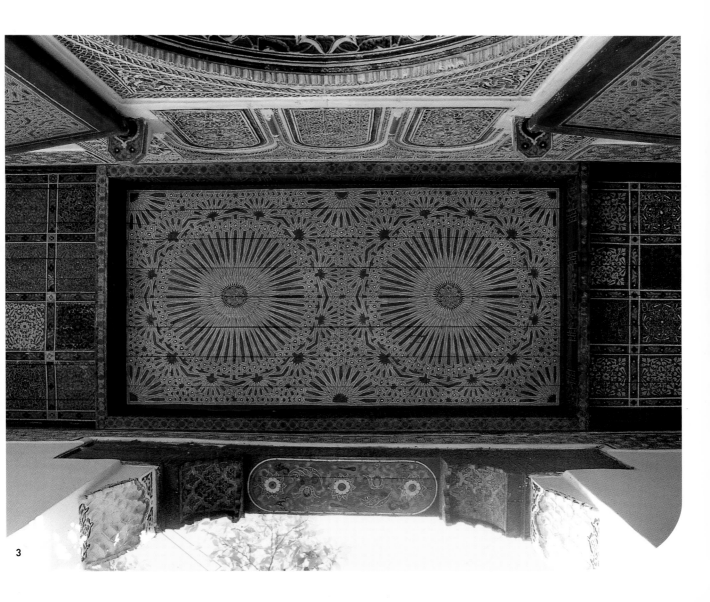

2

3

BENCHES

Low benches are positioned around the entire perimeter of the salon, and can accommodate many people at once. Covered with heavy cotton, velvet or luxurious fabrics, these long and colorful benches are arrayed with a multitude of shimmering cushions.

Generally speaking, the benches are placed on a support made of brick and clay, but they are sometimes also positioned on a cement base covered with *tadelakt* (a type of waterproof wash, see chapter on "Bathrooms") or with *zellige* tiles. The benches are of masonry, no doubt because furniture was quite sparse in traditional Moroccan houses. Most large furniture shops and department stores carry divan-beds or "opium beds," and small cushions at reasonable prices.

You can also reproduce the oriental bench effect by placing a single bed in your living room, covered with a silky fabric and cushions, embroidered and/or decorated with trim. The advantage of this solution is that your bench can be transformed into a bed at a moment's notice. To make sure the cushions do not sag too easily, it is best to choose a dense foam fill (between twenty-four and thirty-one kg/m^3) that is firm and yet comfortable, so that they can instantly bounce back into shape.

Previous page:

1, 2 and 3 In the living room, the place of hospitality par excellence, benches are the key elements of the decor.

FIREPLACES

In the living room the furniture is arranged around a fireplace that can sometimes reach monumental proportions, which vary depending on the dimensions of the room. A decorative element, the fireplace also serves as a source of heat on cool evenings. It is generally made to measure by specialist craftsmen. Very often its frame combines clay bricks, *tadelakt,* and chiseled cedarwood in order to fit in with the surrounding decor.

If you would like a custom-made fireplace that is original, personalized and of fine workmanship, you will most probably need to call upon the services of a professional fireplace installer, who will design and complete your project within the applicable building norms.

In older apartments fireplaces have rarely been taken out but simply covered over. You can simply restore them, adding perhaps a new mantelpiece. The amount of work involved will depend on the state of the hearth and the chimney. If the old hearth is cracked, repair it with refracting cement.

You can find a wide range of fireplace kits as well in Do-it-yourself or home renovation stores (e.g. B&Q), allowing you to create a surround out of brick, stone, or reconstituted stone, depending on your taste.

A concrete fireplace frame could more easily be covered in *tadelakt.*

1, 2 and 3 A fireplace serves as an ideal source of heat for the brief cool season. Made of *tadelakt* and clay brick, it can take any number of fanciful shapes.

MOUCHARABY

Made of cedar, ebony or mahogany wood, the
moucharaby is a typical element of the Moroccan home.
It is a latticed screen composed of turned, sculpted and
interlaced wooden rods that form small octagonal or
star-shaped openings. Placed before the windows, they
preserve a degree of privacy and welcome shade, while
letting in the fresh air when the heat is oppressive. In
former times they also served to allow women to look
out the windows without being seen. There are also
similar works of wooden "lace" on the railings that line
the patios, on the screens of the *medersas* (religious
schools), on certain doors and room dividers. The style
of decoration on the *moucharaby* is now applied as well
to smaller items of furniture such as tea tables, stools,
and other chairs.

Fez and Meknes are the major centers of production of
the *moucharaby*. The artisans there continue to produce
veritable works of art in wood for domestic interiors,

attesting that the dynamism of this traditional craft is not
linked solely to the tourist trade.

Very practical as a way of dividing up the space within
a large living room or breaking up the monotony of a
bare wall, the screen can lend an air of refinement to
the decor. In a small apartment, for instance, it is useful
to be able to set off a corner as a temporary guest room.
All sorts of screens may be found—in metal, wrought
iron or wood, latticed like a cloister grille, covered
with fabric or made of panels of painted wood (see list
of shops and mail order services at the back). If you
enjoy bargain-hunting, you can also look for screens
in antique and flea markets.

Or you can make one yourself, using wooden panels
or a metal structure that you can cover with the fabric
of your choice.

1 Monumental *moucharaby* door.
  The space remaining between the
  architecture and the door allows for
  a natural ventilation of the rooms.
2 Detail of the star-shaped openings
  of a *moucharaby*.

LEATHER POUFS

Solid or multicolored, cubical, round or rectangular, leather poufs share the space of the salon with the other pieces of furniture. They are handsewn, embroidered with silk thread or decorated with strips of colored leather, and serve both as occasional tables and as additional seating. These can be found in boutiques that sell Moroccan handicrafts. For a smaller room, it is best to choose low furniture (avoid heavy wardrobes) that enhance the feeling of space.

3 A pouf of colored leather, decorated with leather strips, can serve as a small table on occasion.

4 Mother-of-pearl as well as bone and horn can be included in the elaboration of complex geometrical or floral motifs inlaid in the furniture.

INLAID FURNITURE

Thuya, a hard, dark wood, is particularly widespread in the region of Essaouira. Since it has a tendency to splinter while drying, it is rarely used in architecture or for large sculptures. It is used instead to build small pieces of furniture such as low, round tables, chests, boxes, trays and frames, and all kinds of small decorative objects. Wander down below the town ramparts and you will find the renowned artisans who specialize in the inlaying of mother-of-pearl, ivory, and precious woods like lemon and ebony. The ancient art of marquetry was, however, originally developed in Fez.

The Kitchen

URBAN DINNERWARE | RUSTIC DINNERWARE | TAGINES |

FAIENCE TILES | THE COUNTERTOP

Kitchens—both working and living spaces—have always been the exclusive domain of Moroccan women. Here, delicious ancestral recipes are passed down from generation to generation; mothers share with their children the secrets of heady spices, delicate grains, and fine tagines. They know by heart the most refined culinary preparations, which they lay out with care on large platters of glazed pottery. On holidays the kitchen reverberates with laughter, animated conversations, and exchanges of recipes. In feverish excitement, relatives, friends, and neighbors pitch in while tempting aromas rise from the pots and tagines during the cooking. In the upper parts of the couscoussiers the grains expand from the steam while, in the lower part, the meat, and vegetables simmer. Nearby, the spices are ground in a stone mortar, ready to be added to the dish at the appropriate moment.

Luminous, spacious, and sparsely furnished, the kitchen is filled primarily with the basic cooking utensils: different sizes of cauldrons and saucepans in stainless steel or copper, with a kettle full of boiling water for tea at any moment, fine urban dinnerware for sumptuous meals, along with everyday rustic ware. Simple, functional accessories contribute to the pleasure of meal preparation and daily living in this, the focal point of the Moroccan house.

URBAN TABLEWARE

For a long time two kinds of ceramics have co-existed in Morocco: one a simple, rustic pottery decorated with natural dyes, and the other a finer, and far more exclusive, enameled ceramic. The former, widespread in the Rif mountains (in the massif of Zerhoun) is commonly known as Berber pottery. The latter, with its delicate designs and shapes, was developed in the cities of Fez, Meknes, Salé and Safi.

The undisputed city of art, Fez is the capital of faience. Its production of ceramics, sometimes in a blue pattern and sometimes polychrome, remains unequalled. The artisans, subsequently establishing themselves in Meknes (around the eighteenth century), and then in Safi, had originally come from this imperial city. Whether in the form of dishes, vases or perfume bottles, these objects are recognizable by the elegance of their shapes, the intricacy of their design and the harmony of their colors. The palette of these master potters consists of four colors: green, yellow, brown, and blue. This last,

a clear, purplish tone made of purified cobalt oxide, occupies pride of place in the ceramics of Fez.

The stylized floral motifs, patterns of lozenges or star polygons likewise have their origins in the classical repertoire of Moroccan-Andalusian architectural art and furniture. The clay, the raw material, undergoes various stages of mixing, kneading, and fermentation before being divided into lumps to be shaped on the wheel. The objects dry in the open air and undergo an initial firing. They are then dipped in white enamel, and, once dry, they can be decorated with a handheld paintbrush in a range of colorful motifs: jasmine flowers, pomegranate seeds, acanthus leaves, palms, and rosettes. Only after that comes the second firing, that of the enamels which will enhance their splendid colors. After Fez, Safi is the second most important center for ceramics. Very deeply imprinted by the Fassie influence, the artisans of the Atlantic coast have also developed their own unique style. Utilizing traditional colors—

1

2

3

blue, yellow, green, brown—they are able to create curved designs, neither linear nor floral, of a perfect symmetry. They prefer the technique of enamel under-glazing to the enamel of Fez; the design is first painted on a clay base before receiving a transparent glaze. Salé, near Rabat, is blessed with a very malleable clay soil. Its ceramics, adorned with beautifully symmetrical garlands of flowers and bouquets in pastel tones—pale blue, rose, and green—are shapely and solid. To meet the demand, the traditional production, with Berber and Andalusian motifs, is gradually being adapted to Western tastes. It is very easy to find this kind of fine tableware in craft boutiques.

In Marrakesh they have recently been producing colored dinnerware along contemporary lines (Atelier Akkal). Everyday objects have been reexamined and simpler, plain, and elegant forms are being created. Tagines, plates, and tea services in solid colors enliven tables and bring a new dynamic to Moroccan creativity. They can be found in several London design and home furnishing boutiques (Pier, Talisman Trading Company).

1 Patterns of blue lozenges are typical of Fez pottery.
2 Dinnerware of contemporary design produced at Marrakesh.
3 and 4 The production of enameled ceramics in delicate designs was developed mainly in the cities of Fez, Meknes, Salé and Safi.

RUSTIC DINNERWARE

In the rural areas, Berber pottery (in ocher earthen-ware) with its simple curves, decorated with archaic red and black motifs, is to be found in every home. Crafted on a potter's wheel by men or molded by hands by women, its basic purpose is domestic use. The sober, functional lines make this family tableware easy to use. Women make frequent use of jars, amphorae, large straight-edged platters, narrow-mouthed pots, pitchers, and tagines. The most beautiful pieces originate in northern Morocco, from the Rif region, and from certain villages in the south. They are decorated with irregular geometric motifs, traced with the help of a handheld brush made of goat or donkey hair. The potters use natural pigments for painting crosses, lozenges, squares, and traditional checkerboard patterns. Once the ideal number of objects has been reached, the firing is arranged in a rudimentary kiln made of heat-resistant bricks, maintained at around 1000° C for many hours (between six and twenty-four hours depending on the type of object). Then follows a slow cooling in a hermetically sealed oven. This kind of pottery is widely available at local markets but is rarely sold beyond its region of origin.

1 In the foreground a rustic pitcher made with simple curves and archaic motifs. The most beautiful pieces come from the Rif mountain area and certain villages of the south.

2 Soap dish and pot in terra-cotta in sober lines.

3 The tagine, a dish emblematic of Moroccan cuisine, takes its name from the pot in which it is cooked: a round casserole in glazed earthen-ware topped by a cone-shaped lid.

TAGINES

In every Moroccan house delectable tagines are served in the dishes after which they are named. The recipe includes infinite variations from one region and one family to the next. The kitchen often contains stacks of glazed earthenware dishes of different sizes. Circular in shape, with raised edges, they are covered with cone-shaped lids that enhance the braising process. Thus the heat is well distributed to all the ingredients, which simmer for a long time in the cooking dish, for the true secret of a successful tagine is very slow cooking. During a festive meal, the tagine is brought from the kitchen to the living room in another, bigger dish of identical shape but made of copper or brass, with the one fitting inside the other. When cooking outdoors, the tajine is placed on little barbecues called canouns. In certain more traditional villages the women still cook over charcoal.

If you want to cook in a tagine, the dish will tolerate almost any kind of heat (gas, ceramic, and electric elements), as long as it isn't subjected to sudden changes in temperature. Equip yourself with an earthenware tagine, brown and thickly glazed—not with a decorated one with painted motifs, which is unsuitable for cooking (available in Moroccan craft stores).

1 Berber decoration on this kitchen buffet displaying tagines and traditional baskets.

FAIENCE TILES

Strong, waterproof and easy to maintain, wall tiles are also valued for their decorative qualities.

The most exposed spots are found behind the sink, around the cooking appliances and on the countertop. At these locations, natural terra-cotta is not suitable because of its porosity. However, the bright colors of the enameled earthenware, totally waterproof, can serve equally well for the walls. Enameled faience, too fragile to be used on floors, is ideal for walls. For one thing, it has the advantage of not being susceptible to either stains or detergents and does not become discolored over time. Furthermore, it is available in a wide variety of colors and designs, with either matte or shiny finishes, smooth or textured. You can brighten up a two-toned design (yellow and green) by highlighting it with a decorative border.

WALL TILES

Any amateur is perfectly capable of tiling a wall. Before beginning, check that the wall is level, using a ruler and a level. If the wall has been painted, clean it thoroughly and sand it down to improve adhesion.

An old layer of tile is also a good support, as long as it has been thoroughly cleaned. Pick tiles of a different size from the original ones, so that the joints of the new tiles will overlap the old ones.

Always begin at the bottom of the wall. With decorated tiles you need to start at an angle, the pattern being the crucial factor. The choice of grout will depend on the type of support. To avoid problems, follow manufacturers' instructions. For a considerable savings in time, you might consider using self-adhesive tiles, which are very easy to apply.

Finally, to keep the tiles bright, rub them occasionally with a half-lemon, and then dry them with a cloth.

THE COUNTERTOP

In the kitchen, the countertop is subjected to all kinds of abuse: scrapes, heat, humidity, detergents. It therefore has to be strong as well as attractive. Tile or mosaic made of glass or faience (see the chapter on bathrooms), is particularly suitable to the demands made on these surfaces. Moreover, tiling techniques for a horizontal countertop are very similar to those for a wall. Only the joints require a slightly different treatment: you must use a rubber trowel, filling them right to the surface of the tiles in order to avoid creating grooves where dirt and germs can accumulate. Choose a grout that is moisture-proof, anti-fungal, and resistant (Do-it-yourself stores), because it will have to be cleaned frequently and with very strong products like bleach, which kills germs and mold. If you have to cut more than half a dozen tiles, a cutting jib will be more efficient than tile-cutters. A special abrasive saw, will be helpful when cutting along curves as it permits you to saw along the exact lines.

You can also change the general aspect of the kitchen, without great cost or too much effort, by painting your old tiles. All you need to do is to scrape the surface of the tile with medium sand paper and then pass a damp sponge over it. Apply a primer (Do-it-yourself stores), making sure it is even. Let it dry, and then apply the paint.

1 Outdoor kitchen featuring several stoves designed for cooking on a wood fire. You can see the oven used for baking bread and for mechouis (barbecues).
2 The preparation of the meal takes place on a brick countertop. The stove and cooking table are of terra-cotta brick.

The Dining Area

THE TABLE | LANTERNS | TRAYS

Dining areas as separate living spaces seem to be a relatively recent addition to Moroccan domestic life. Introduced under the French Protectorate (1912-1956), they are not a traditional feature of rural Moroccan houses, where meals are enjoyed in the living room or on benches around low tables.

During the Protectorate General Louis-Hubert Lyautey, the first Resident General, however, instituted a new administration, which represented an important economic initiative and promoted a wave of European immigration. Nearly 40,000 people moved to Morocco, bringing their way of life and the furniture that was all the rage at that time: Art Deco. These innovations influenced the way people thought of their homes, as each room now had a certain function: you cooked in the kitchen, ate in the dining room, and entertained in the living room.

But times have changed. Today, under the influence of Western trends, people have meals in the kitchen or on the main patio. Increasingly, the living room and the dining room are being replaced by one spacious area, which is just as comfortable, and where people like to gather. An intimate atmosphere prevails, encouraging conversation and conviviality. People get together to eat, drink tea, and catch up with friends and family. The dining room has become the central nervous system of a house.

THE TABLE

If you do not have enough space to create a real dining area, you can opt for an adjustable living room table that can be adapted to your needs and wishes, in a low position in front of a sofa, or raised up higher for meals. There are also folding tables which, when folded, serve as consoles. All you need to do is set them up on the days you are entertaining. If your living room lacks space but is where you usually have your meals, set up a round table. It will be less intrusive than a square or rectangular one. If the room permits it, consider extensions to accommodate guests.

In a large living room divided into several areas, the windows should determine the positioning of the table. It will be placed in the natural light so as to avoid artificial lighting during daytime. To add an oriental touch to your table, cover it with bright, embroidered tablecloths you have found in the souks or in the boutiques carrying Moroccan crafts.

1 Table set for tea.
2 The tables and chairs in this beautiful dining area date from the 1930s.

1

In good weather, it is not unusual for the main patio to become the place of choice for the hosts of a *riad* to gather at mealtime around a table placed beneath a cascade of bougainvillea, seated on wrought iron chairs. This material is a very popular decorative element in dining area furnishings, for it follows pure, modern lines. One finds it used for chairs, table feet, consoles, or mirrors. Created by artisans, it embodies the beauty and the richness of their ancestral *savoir faire* (see the section on "Wrought iron grilles" in the chapter on Patios and Terraces).

For a dining area that does not have much daylight, choose bright colors for the walls. Tones of ocher-yellow, for example, will add brightness and catch the light, creating an illusion of space.

1 Detail of Moroccan decoration on earthenware.
2 Detail of Moroccan pouf and carpet for a dining area-salon combination.
3 On a table signed by Quentin Wilbaux, one can see the contemporary dishes of Charlotte Barkowski.

LANTERNS

Essential accessories in Morocco, lanterns and storm
lanterns are to be found everywhere in the *riads*.
At twilight, their little glowing rays dot the roof terraces, galleries, and patios. The darker it gets, the
more their gentle light enhances the nooks and cran-
nies of the house, from bedrooms to the salon, up and
down the staircases. You can't help succumbing to
the magic of these lanterns with their tinted glass and
metal filigree.
Recreate this profusion of tiny sources of light by placing lanterns here and there—on furniture or window
sills, where they will contribute to a friendly ambiance.
Make sure the lighting is neither too bright nor too
low. On the dining room table it should be strong
enough to see what is on the plates, and the candle
flames ought to be positioned below the eye level of
the guests.

1 and 3 As night falls, rays of glowing
lanterns in metal and colored
glass create a warm and pleasing light.
2 Mint tea is served on finely
engraved trays.

TRAYS

In the tumult of the souks the rhythmic sound of
hammering signals the workshops of the metalworkers
who transform copper, bronze, brass, and German
silver (an alloy resembling silver) into a variety of
objects. The constant hammer blows shape and form
the sheets of copper into shiny golden brown trays.
Delicately chiseled with geometric or floral designs,
the platters rub shoulders with incense burners,
lanterns and huge cauldrons.
When it is time for mint tea, the ladies of the house
take great pride in offering tiny glasses of the sweet
liquid and a wide array of pastries on ornate, engraved
trays. This decorative accessory, widely available, is
easy to find (see stores listed at the end of the book).

The Bedroom

RURAL CARPETS | URBAN CARPETS | MATS | FABRICS | *TATAOUI* | LIMEWASH |

PIGMENTS | ADOBE BRICK

Between Spain and the western Maghreb, a constant flow of cultural, social, and commercial exchanges over many centuries gave rise to an extremely rich art, the most beautiful accomplishments of which may be seen in Morocco. From the eleventh century on, with the rise of the Almoravid dynastsy, the region saw a veritable Hispanization of Moroccan architecture and culture. The traces of this fabulous Arabo-Andalusian symbiosis are still felt throughout the country today. You just need to wander through the heart of the imperial cities and enter one of the *riads* to see for yourself. Hidden behind the blind walls of the *medinas*, these architectural jewels still bear the marks of this dual origin: polychrome faience mosaics on the floor and walls, chiselled stucco ornamentation, and painted or sculpted wood.

The rooms are organized according to a standard pattern, around a more or less vast patio surrounded by porticoes and a basin or pool at the center. On the ground floor and upstairs, the living spaces (*bayt*) take up an entire side of the courtyard and do not communicate with each other. You have to return to the patio or walk along the galleries to go from one room to the next.

Inside the rooms a beneficent semi-obscurity reigns. The amount of natural light depends to a considerable extent on the size of the doors and windows, which open exclusively onto the patio. With the most exquisite gentleness, the fabrics, drapery, and carpets—be they simple or elaborate—preserve the reassuring atmosphere of the Muslim home. The cedarwood furniture, the sun-baked terra-cotta and the ocher tones on the walls contribute greatly to this sense of well-being. Now for a guided tour of these most private dwelling-places that celebrate, whether with pomp or simplicity, a refined oriental way of life.

RURAL CARPETS

In Morocco, all homes have carpets. Whether deep- or short-pile, with simple or complex motifs, large or small, rural or urban, the carpets lend their warmth to absolutely every Moroccan interior. Their warm and lively colors brighten the most luxurious palaces as well as the most rudimentary Berber tents, by way of the most austere casbahs. The Berber rugs are very thick, and were designed by the nomadic tribes to protect themselves from the cold. They are tailored to the dimensions of the tents and can also be used for sleeping. In the eastern Middle Atlas mountains, these carpets of great beauty are predominantly ecru in color, decorated with brown or black geometric patterns. But the most renowned are those of the Ouarzazate region. Long and narrow to fit the rooms of the casbahs, they are generally dark red, illuminated with saffron yellow and orange, and have a central motif. Other geometric designs—triangles, squares, lozenges, and broken lines—enrich the esthetic appeal of these utilitarian objects produced in great simplicity.

URBAN CARPETS

Almost always adorned with floral, animal, and geometric motifs, urban carpets take their inspiration from the oriental rugs imported into Morocco in the eighteenth century. Strongly permeated by Arab and Eastern influences, their designs combine a variety of complex forms. The most highly esteemed are the carpets of Rabat, bright red, brick or antique rose in color: around a central medallion in the shape of a lozenge, star or rosette, a multitude of triangular designs and concentric bands cascade right out to the edges. A typical element of urban carpets, the borders are abundantly decorated with floral and geometric designs. Whether placed on the floor or hung on the wall, these sumptuous carpets are particularly useful for marking off the different zones of a large room, while at the same time lending the space a sense of great warmth.

1 and 2 Whether deep- or short-piled, with complex or simple motifs, rural or urban, carpets are on display in every room of the house.
3 The floor in this tribal chief's tent is covered entirely with urban-style carpets.

MATS

In Moroccan cities and the countryside, basket weaving is a very widespread popular craft that is generally carried out in the open air. On the one hand, space is needed to produce the larger objects (pergolas, smaller furniture, baskets). On the other, they hope that the items, usually for domestic use, might be sold as soon as they are finished. The basket makers weave these household objects out of reeds, palm leaves, and esparto grass, while the mat makers use rushes to make the large mats that cover the floors of domestic interiors and mosques. These coverings of vegetable fibers blend harmoniously with the floors and walls made from raw materials (clay brick, adobe, lime, terra-cotta tiles).

1 Headboard and night table in woven vegetable fibers.
2 and 4 Rooms decorated in solid or multicolored fabrics reflect a way of life shot through with Arabo-Andalusian influences.
3 Two-toned mat, made of rushes woven together with linen.

FABRICS

Moroccans have always demonstrated a very sharp esthetic sense in the field of textiles. Endowed with an unusual talent for combining textures, motifs, and especially colors, they have a keen eye for beautiful fabrics, which play a privileged role in decorating salons and bedrooms. The latter, hung with monochrome or multicolored cotton, silk, brocade or muslin cloth, reflect a refined art of living permeated with oriental, Andalusian and Berber influences.

Damask and brocade are fine textiles that recall the Orient and can be used to make majestic curtains. The former, in reversible monochrome silk, has a matte design on a shiny background, whereas the latter is decorated with rich designs in relief. Both sport very vivid colors: antique red, gold, and creamy beige. Brocade produces a greater effect, for instance as a tablecloth with large overhang for a special event.

If you wish to make your own shiny cushions or elegant, soft curtains, upholstery fabrics such as silk bourrette, which is slightly matte and irregular, or a shiny and smooth satin are ideally suited. For a more ethnic look, a Berber blanket in striped multicolored linen can make a very good bedspread.

1 Bits of Moroccan embroidery dot this fabric tieback.
2 A piece of ecru cloth is hung from a curtain rod to create the effect of drapery, accompanied by large tassled tiebacks.

1

MAKING A TENT

To produce the effect of a tent, a very simple way of transforming your space is to hang some fabric from curtain rods (available at fabric or hardware stores as well as any major department or home furnishings store) to form several folds. The edges sweep the ground on either side of the bed.

The fabric can also be used as a drapery and hung across the full length of the walls. To get a thicker effect, count three times the width of the wall when buying the fabric. Large spaces can accommodate cotton sheeting, voile or muslin, all of which are inexpensive. Hung in this way, they can easily be taken down and machine-washed. More costly fabrics are generally reserved for smaller spaces.

Copper piping is both decorative and practical for hanging drapery, and the polished brown metal adds a further oriental touch to the decor.

TATAOUI

In southern Morocco, the adobe casbahs and ksours, with their elegant guard towers alongside, dominate the pre-Saharan valleys and hold many surprises for the attentive visitor. Clay is the dominant material in these rows of attached buildings, but raise your eyes and you will see that the ceilings are covered with tinted laurel branches.

The word *tataoui* designates a traditional technique for making ceilings that has great decorative value. Its origin is in the south, more specifically from the Tata wadi, a tributary of the Drâa, the shores of which are covered in wild laurel. The laurel is cut into wooden rods, then boiled in dyed water. Once dry, the rods are arranged in squares or lozenge shapes on joists of poplar, thuya or palm logs. Above, a layer of thick branches, held in place with a mixture of moist earth, lime, sand, straw, and ash, serves to render the surface waterproof. This technique, which helps bring color to rural dwellings that are otherwise often quite spartan, has now spread throughout the country and can easily be exported. It is used by contemporary decorators to cover the ceilings of *riads*, villas, and hotels, to the point that the term *tataoui* is now widely used to refer to all ceilings decorated in vegetable fibers (reeds, bamboo, palm branches, etc.).

1 The beauty of the painted ceiling is enhanced by the sober, natural tones of this room.
2 and 3 Tinted laurel rods, shaped into lozenges and triangles, form the decorative patterns of these *tataoui* ceilings.

LIMEWASH

Lime is a natural binding agent for washes applied to clay brick. Both inside and outside, it respects and enhances the thermal quality of the walls (which help regulate the termperature). Easy to handle, it can be applied without difficulty and adheres well to natural surfaces. Healthy, tough, and inexpensive, it has a structural flexibility that allows it to tolerate sudden changes in temperature without cracking. As it can be reused endlessly, none of it goes to waste. Highly absorbent, it also has a disinfectant and fungicidal quality. Since it is highly compatible with natural materials, it can be mixed with various clay pigments. Limewash can also be applied to stone, cellular concrete or cinder block. For any other base, a diluted vinyl glue or acrylic binding agent will need to be added.

To paint on a limewashed wall, prepare the surface by applying a coating (Do-it-yourself stores) with more or less relief depending on the texture desired, and then apply three layers of lime with a graining brush, in twenty-four hour intervals. Or use limewash available in the form of a ready-to-use paste (e.g. from Mike Wye and Associates), and dilute it in water (three parts to one part lime) with a mixer or a drill that has a mixer attachment. Untinted, the resulting coat is almost transparent: which is why several thin layers need to be applied.

To tint the lime, dilute pigment powder in a little water (no more than 20% of the weight of the lime) to get a smooth paste and add a drop of liquid soap or alcohol to help disperse the pigment in the water. Then add this mixture to the lime, taking care to note the quantities used in case you need to make some more later. Apply the lime to the walls with a large brush. The intensity of the color diminishes after it has dried, and hence several coats will be necessary. For a cloudy effect, use a graining brush, then stipple with a sponge or cloth. On the interior walls limewash has considerable longevity.

The same powdery effect can also be obtained with a casein-based wash (casein is a protein extracted from milk), which has very attractive features—it has good coverage, is very matte, easy to use and saturates the colors well. For some time now, certain paint stores have websites (e.g. Johnstone's) that let you preview your projects on the computer. All you need to do is to select a room that resembles yours, choose the color you would like, and apply it by clicking on the virtual walls. For exteriors covered in lime, the wash can be obtained by mixing one part lime with two parts water. For an attractive result, apply three layers in twenty-four hour intervals. This wash needs to be renewed every ten years in order to preserve its sparkling whiteness. But this will of course depend on local climate conditions.

In northern Morocco lime mixed with natural pigments and linseed oil is applied to the magnificent walls of, for example, the *medinas* of Tétouan, Essaouira and Tanger.

FINISH

To prepare a good, smooth surface, use a fairly large knife. But make sure not to create any excessive thickness, which would require sanding afterwards. Remember that it is easier to go back and fill in any areas where there may be insufficient thickness. If the knife leaves a "mustache," just remove it after drying.

1 Geometric motifs in natural pigments decorate this limewashed wall.

PIGMENTS

Very often in northern Morocco the base of the walls is decorated with geometric or floral patterns (the same as those found on carpets, pottery, etc.) colored with pigments. Ideal for tinting paint, patina, and finishes, natural pigments can produce very subtle tones.

It is best to mix them with other powders such as plaster or lime, rather than adding them directly to the paint or ready-to-use finishes, since this might make them grainy.

It is also useful to know that white acrylic paint atten-uates the intensity of the dyes. For a deep color on an acrylic base, it is strongly recommended that you dilute the pigments in a bit of water, which you then add to an acrylic binding agent. To find the right dosage for the colors, test them first on a small surface, since the hue can turn very much lighter after drying.

Apply the white paint to the wall, followed by a layer of this mixture with a regular or a graining brush. You can add a second layer if necessary, or add a coat of varnish to protect the paint.

After use, the pigment powders must be kept stored free from humidity.

1 Natural pigments can be used to obtain very intense tones, such as on the red walls of this room.

ADOBE BRICK

Adobe, an ancient building material, refers to the production of raw, molded bricks dried in the sun. The clay-like earth, to which straw is sometimes added, is moistened to form a sort of paste. This is poured into a wooden mold, then turned out with a brisk movement, and the molded earth is then left to dry for a few days. The adobe bricks are then turned over to ensure that they dry evenly. After they have dried, they are ready to be used in a masonry structure. In Morocco it is not unusual for adobe bricks to be made of earth found on the construction site itself.

To reinforce the walls and corners, window openings and vaults, the only way to increase the resistance of bricks was to fire them. Fired bricks were thus used as a harmonious supplement to a structure in adobe. For the floor, generally *bejmate* is used, a mechanically baked brick that is less porous. The latter is often used on patios and in the interior spaces of the *riads*.

2 In Morocco, there is renewed enthusiasm for raw bricks. They can be used to create more complex structures.

3 Brick cupola in clay pierced with oculi, small circular openings filled with glass.

RAW BRICK

In brick architecture, both traditional and contemporary, raw bricks are also used as decorative elements. Their distinctive form of masonry provides a type of decoration in relief, using simple patterns such as lozenges, chevrons, lines, etc. These motifs are especially brought out by the subtle play of light and shadow that caresses the earthen texture of the walls. Recently, the passion for the natural elegance of raw brick has led to its use to form curved structures such as arches, faults, and cupolas that until then had been made of fired bricks.

The Bathroom

TADELAKT | THE HAMMAM | ZELLIGE TILES | MOSAICS

To this day Moroccans regard the bath as a communal meeting place. On Fridays, the day of great prayer, crowds fill the hammams. "The cleanliness of the body is as important as the purity of the soul," the muezzin reminds the faithful in his entrancing chant. The function of the hammam as a place of collective purification explains its importance in Muslim cities. Yet in North Africa, where these encounters in the steam have survived better than anywhere else, it is not just out of necessity but also for the sheer pleasure of it that people take to the communal baths. These are especially popular among women, who regard them as places of conviviality and social networking. The baths of the Maghreb cannot rival the luxurious beauty of those of the Orient; they are simple in construction and privilege the functional over the esthetic.

Just like prayer, ablutions are also communal in nature, but, of course, men and women always bathe separately, attending on the days and times reserved for them. The system of these "Moorish baths," dividing the spaces into hot, warm and cold rooms, is inspired directly by the baths of the Roman era.

In private houses, the bathroom is likewise a space reserved for washing, personal hygiene and the pleasures of water. Given its exposure to humidity and splashing, *zellige* tiles and a *tadelakt* finish seem to be the most suitable wall coverings. Allow yourself to be seduced by the comfort and refinement of these places of delight.

TADELAKT

The word comes from the Arab verb *dlek*, which means "to massage." It is a kind of plaster made of pure lime, originally from Marrakesh, that is sifted and mixed with a natural pigment, moistened, and then kneaded at length. Applied as a roughcast finish on a rough surface, it is subsequently rubbed down to a produce a fine, smooth layer. Its luster is obtained by means of a second paste, made of egg yolks and a black polishing soap (one kg of soap for fifty to one hundred eggs, depending on the desired richness of the mixture), that brings out its sheen and produces a veined effect. The *tadelakt* is then polished and reinforced with a smooth stone. It is the process of polishing the surface inch by inch that gives *tadelakt* its distinctive appearance. The waterproof quality of *tadelakt* makes it the finish of choice for hammams and other public baths. Its smooth texture allows condensation to trickle down the walls, sparing the bathers the inconvenience of cold water dripping down on them. To avoid the veined effect, it is now common to leave out the eggs and to add an extra coat of soap. The substance is much appreciated for its longevity and the variety of colors available, and hence the use of *tadelakt* for decorative purposes has been extended to the salons, bedrooms, and of course the bathroom. Even if this skill remains closely linked to Marrakesh, there are inexpensive ready-to-use versions available in a variety of colors (Tierrafino Stone, Mike Wye & Associates). These are quite easy to apply and Tierrafino provides online documentation as well as weekend workshops in *tadelakt* technique in various places in Britain and Europe.

1, 2 , 3 and 4 Much appreciated for its sheen, its veined effect and its resistance to water, *tadelakt* has also come to be used on basins, showers, and bathtubs.

2

3

Tadelakt is applied on solid, hard bases of brick, cement or stone, and over just about any irregular finish of a lime, cement, and sand base.

Since it is the treatment with black soap that makes it waterproof, it is important to apply this properly with a cloth, and within twenty-four hours of having applied the finish. One person cannot cover more than three to four m² per day. Two or more people will be needed to do larger surfaces.

Since it takes four months for the substance to dry fully and reach its definitive resistance, you must take this into account when using it in bathrooms. It is therefore recommended that great care be taken during the first two months, since it hardens only gradually. To make sure your *tadelakt* does not deteriorate over time, wash it with black soap and do not use any scouring cream or descaling products. It is a good idea to grease surfaces that are subject to much wear and tear (baths, basins) once a month with black soap.

THE HAMMAM

Formerly, the wealth of a city was measured by the beauty and luxuriousness of its hammams. Muslim architects were not considered to have been truly initiated into their craft until they had finished building a hammam. Heirs to the Roman baths, the buildings generally follow the classic Andalusian layout adopted from the eleventh century. The three rooms (cold, warm, and hot) and often even the resting room open on to one another. Cupolas allow some scant daylight to pass through, filtered by bottleneck-shaped openings known as *oculi*. For Moroccan women who spend hours on end at the baths, the time represents an ideal parenthesis between daily chores—a welcome moment of leisure in a busy life. If the city women appreciate the convenience of private bathrooms, they nevertheless continue to visit the little neighborhood hammams. In this atmosphere, clouded with mist, their silhouettes move about carrying wooden pails, the sound of their wooden sandals knocking on the burning marble floors. Each

person helps the other in the various stages of bathing: massage, rubbing down, combing out long hair, varnishing nails, make-up, etc. The women apply ointments and oils, perfumes, *rassoul* (a mineral-rich mud) and honey-based creams to each other, while the vapor permeates every nook and cranny of the hot room.

Even if you are short of space, you can reproduce this center of relaxation and pleasure at home by placing a steam machine and a waterproof door in your shower stall to create a steam room. In this way, you will be able to treat yourself to the beneficent effects of water condensation. If you opt for this solution, the walls will have to be entirely waterproof (covered entirely by tiles or *tadelakt*).

1 A sheer curtain in which women wrap themselves, called a *haik*, can be used to conceal the shower stall.
2 The walls of the hammams are covered with *tadelakt*, a mixture of lime from Marrakesh and natural pigments.
3 During a hammam session, bathers sprinkle themselves with cold water from wooden pails known as *kebabs*.

ZELLIGE TILES

Introduced to Morocco by the Almohad dynasty (eleventh to twelfth centuries), ceramic marquetry was first used to decorate the upper levels of the minarets (such as the one at Koutoubia). This decorative technique was used widely during the following century in Nasrid Spain and in Morocco under the Merinids and was eventually applied widely not only to minarets but also to walls, columns, and floors. It is widely used in the *medersas* (Islamic schools), palaces, and homes. *Zellige* tiles are used to decorate walls, the courtyard pavements, pillars around the patio and wall fountains. To this day the art of *zellige* mosaics perpetuates the medieval Islamic esthetic forms in architecture and on traditional furniture. Drawing inspiration from the decorative repertoire of Andalusia at the time of the Merinids and the Nasrids, artisans have nonetheless added some novel elements taken from the Orient or brought from Moorish Spain by Morisco emigrés. At Tétouan, for instance, a Moorish style of *zelliges* continues to be popular, and constitutes one of the city's specialties. The process involves cutting up small pieces of ceramics before they are glazed. It is perfectly possible to create a decor with *zellige* tiles, sold in England and elsewhere in squares or on a net backing (Dar Interiors, Habibi Interiors). It is probably best to draw on the expertise of a professional for applying these sublime decorative surfaces. The technique of *zellige* consists of juxtaposing tiny pieces of enameled pottery in order to compose a strict geometric design. Each monochrome ceramic fragment is cut into a triangle, lozenge, trapezoid or star shape. The pieces are assembled upside down on a panel and set in a mixture of cement and lime. These decorative panels are then applied to the walls, where they repeat in infinite variety the sparkling motifs of considerable diversity.

Given the complexity of this technique, it is best to hire a professional to carry it out. If you need to tile large surfaces, consider choosing imitation tiles, sold in panels or by squares, for this will mean considerable

1 and 2 The art of *zellige*, or ceramic marquetry, perpetuates the strict geometric designs inherited from the era of the Almohad dynasty. This decorative technique adorns the walls, courtyard pavements, patio pillars and fountains.

AMBIANCE

In the bathrooms, the new generations of enameled tiles that imitate the raw materials (earth, stone, cement, etc.) make it easy to create the seductive ocher ambiance at a very reasonable price.

Moreover, this material is the most suited for surfaces exposed to water, and the walls will remain impeccable for a long time, as long as the joints are regularly maintained.

Tiling is also available that reflects an oriental decor, using mosaics placed side by side without any joints. The surface is then finished with a flexible mortar (Fermajoint).

savings in time. Another alternative: certain tile manufacturers have a tile showroom, which serves as a
veritable documentation center (Dar Interiors, Habib-
Interiors), and offer colored squares of enameled lava
stone measuring thirteen by thirteen cm and made up
of little squares of one by one, as well as pre-assembled
mosaics with which to create friezes of rosettes, star
polygons, interlaced lines, flower sprays, etc. The com-
binations are endless. However, the eight or twelve-
pointed star shape, repeated indefinitely, remains the
most widespread motif in Moroccan houses. Resistant
to the light and to climate changes, these decorative
coverings retain their resistance to humidity and pro-

vide a bit of freshness in the summer. They decorate
almost every room, from living room to patio, by way
of the kitchen and the bathroom.

1 and 2 The ocher walls in *tadelakt*
often serve as a screen to a
bathroom covered in *zelliges*.
3 *Tadelakt* is abundantly used
in bathrooms.

MOSAIC

Whether of enamel, stone or glass, mosaic brings color
and texture to the walls, basins, and other surfaces.
The recipe for easily covering a base, while leaving
free rein to your creativity, is very simple. The technique takes quite long, but it is not as difficult as
you might think. All you need to do is place, with
patience, small pieces of glass mosaic or tiles in a mold.
A jig made of wooden sticks is sometimes necessary to
form a mold, notably for tabletops.

Knead the mortar, composed of three parts cement
and two parts water, to mix with some diluted EVA
glue (two parts water to one part glue) until you get
a thick paste.

Trace the motif you want to create directly onto the
paste by means of a small stick. In the beginning,
choose a simple design. Position the mosaic following
the design. Since certain tiles need to be cut, use a tile
cutter. Let it dry for about twenty-four hours.

1 Detail of traditional mosaic.
2 Golden brown metals such as copper
and tin go very well with the lustered
texture of *tadelakt* or with the mosaics.

Patio and Terrace

WINDOWS | WROUGHT IRON GRILLES | FOUNTAINS | EARTHENWARE JARS |

OUTDOOR FURNITURE | ROOF TERRACES | PLANTS | LIGHTING

In the *hadith* we read that the prophet Mohammed advises against allowing the eyes of strangers to peer into one's house—it is no doubt for this reason that Moroccan cities and houses are hidden behind austere walls. Windows are not very popular and, if tolerated at all, are the size of small skylights, placed high up and covered by a grille. In the narrow streets that twist and turn without any seeming order, the passerby sees only walls. The walls of mosques, palaces, *riads* …. Fortunately, a door sometimes opens onto a zigzag entrance, leading to an open-air courtyard. The contrast is striking between the exterior with its high, blind walls amid the tumultuous streets, and the bright interior filled with a subtle atmosphere of well-being.

Square or rectangular in shape, the courtyard is often adorned by a fountain at the center; it may also be divided into four segments planted with trees and surrounded by a portico made up of three arcades on each side, with the central arcade always the largest and highest. If there is an upper story, the portico of the top floor is identical to that of the lower level. This gallery helps protect the rooms from the sun and the rain. In general, the air is pleasant thanks to the natural ventilation system inherent in this type of construction.

These houses, open at the center, have introduced a habit that endures both in the casbah and in modern-day structures: seasonal mobility. In the summer, the fountain gives off freshness, and so people live on the ground floor and in the evening find refuge on the roof terrace, transformed for the occasion into a living room. In winter, the occupants seek warmth and thus tend to gather in the upstairs rooms that are more exposed to the sun. Such vertical moves, dictated by climate conditions, optimize the use made of these dwellings.

WINDOWS

In the West, windows have three basic functions: the distribution of natural light, fresh air, and to provide a view outside. By contrast, in the introverted architecture of Morocco they are used to control temperature, bring in fresh air, and protect the residents' privacy. The double-hung windows are fitted with heavy interior shutters. These are made of cedar wood, palm, or poplar depending on the region.

The *chemassiates*, small decorative piercings above the doors made of chiseled plaster, favor the evacuation of hot air, which tends to rise.

1 Windows regulate the temperature while safeguarding privacy.
2 and 3 Balustrades in iron lacework witness to the skill of the artisan blacksmith.

WROUGHT IRON GRILLES

In Morocco, the work of blacksmiths draws great admiration. In their workshops, scattered with small pieces of metal, the artisans work on the floor with an anvil held between their legs. In their hands bits of red-hot metal are brought to life, intended to decorate the ornamental grilles of middle-class houses. Their curved lines form elegant vaults and exquisite interlaces in which the Andalusian influence can be seen very clearly. A veritable lace in matte black iron, these railings contrast starkly with the ocher color of the walls. Used for centuries in traditional architecture, wrought iron is increasingly found in Moroccan interiors. The purity of its lines makes it an attractive material for table legs, the backs of chairs, room dividers, balustrades, and banisters. On the windows, wrought iron grilles are gradually replacing the *moucharaby* of carved cedar, and serve the same purpose of safeguarding private spaces. Very beautiful pieces of ironwork can be ordered made to measure in the Moroccan workshops.

1 and 2 The decorative use of wrought
iron has spread throughout the
interiors of houses: armchairs, chairs,
banisters, and chandeliers make use
of its pure lines and scrolls.

3 Wrought iron grilles are gradually
replacing the cedar *moucharaby*
on windows.

4 Monumental grille shelters sophisticated
decors of varying sizes.

FOUNTAINS

In the courtyard, the central fountain, made of marble or covered in *zellige* tiles, is another device for cooling the atmosphere. In summer, when temperatures range between 40 and 45°C and there is no whiff of a breeze, the evaporation of the water brings coolness to the home. Sometimes a fountain extends outward into rivulets and is hooked up to irrigation pipes or to a spring. In wealthy homes, an enclosed garden planted with lemon, orange, fig and pomegranate trees may be added to the central courtyard. Gardening centers offer a large selection of suitable fountains and basins.

1 and 2 Sculpted marble fountains have more than a merely esthetic function: they are also intended to cool the air during times of great heat.
3 In large houses the fountains are often surrounded by basins.

2

EARTHENWARE JARS

For terraces with a southern exposure, earthenware jars are ideal additions, since the water for the plants that they contain evaporates through their porous sides, refreshing the flowerpots and roots. The soil is well aerated and the jars prevent moss from spreading or the roots from suffocating. Choose ocher jars and brighten them up with a few touches of color (brick red, dark green, blue).

Be aware, however, that handmade terra-cotta pots are much more expensive than mass produced ones. Varnished or enameled in rich colors, they are also more fragile, so keep them well away from areas that see a lot of traffic. On account of their porosity, earthenware objects do not like the frost: be sure to put them away in winter, or protect them with a plastic sheet if they are difficult to move. You can also find plastic pots that are matte and coarse in texture, perfectly imitating terra-cotta pottery but so light that they are easily overturned. To protect them from the wind, it is best to position them between heavier objects such as clay pots.

1 Amphorae and terra-cotta jars punctuate this patio decorated with *zellige* tiles.
2 The fountain, placed on an octagonal base decorated with jars, contributes to the refinement of the area.

OUTDOOR FURNITURE

Rotproof, solid, durable and resistant to insect attacks, teak possesses so many good qualities that it has become synonymous with outdoor furniture. As it requires no upkeep, it can stay outdoors but over time will acquire a grey patina.

If you wish to preserve its brown tint, this type of wood must be treated with a special nourishing oil. Begin by dusting or cleaning with steel wool if necessary, and then apply two coats of oil at an interval of eight hours.

If you opt for metal furniture, remember that aluminum requires no special maintenance. If it is thermally coated, the paint is hard although it can scratch, so you should rub it with an automobile polish.

For other metals, whether treated or not, the upkeep is simple: sand any damaged areas and add two coats of anti-rust paint. Finally, don't forget that metal furniture needs to be brought indoors in the cold season.

MOROCCAN SALONS

With just a few blocks of synthetic foam covered with thick cotton and enlivened with cushions, you can create a Moroccan salon, to which you might wish to add a low table. However, be careful when buying the foam: its density, measured in kg/m^3, should be high (thirty-five kg/m^3 at the least), for the higher it is, the more solid it is and of better quality.

1 The patio is an area dedicated to tranquility. Sheltered from the eyes of strangers, it allows for moments of relaxation.

2 Aside from cedar, pine, olive, and beech are the most commonly used kinds of wood in carpentry.

ROOF TERRACES

Far from the indiscreet looks of strangers, terraces constitute additional space, where true relaxation can be found. Since roof terraces are generally more spacious than any other kind, they are ideal for setting up a salon of deck chairs for sunbathing, tea drinking, or dinner with friends.

If the surface of the floor is large, a covering should be found that is both practical and esthetically pleasing. Concrete, contrary to popular belief, is perfectly suited to this double requirement. Rational, practical and inexpensive, it offers a multiplicity of colors, forms and possible imitations (e.g. ancient paving stones) while retaining its robust quality.

A mixture of cement, sand, and gravel, concrete is an ideal material to cover terraces that see a great deal of traffic or bear heavy weight. You can even mix your own out of materials bought separately, or else buy the dry components already mixed in the correct propor-tions, requiring only the addition of water to form a homogeneous paste. The latter solution seems the most practical for pouring concrete into small areas.

For larger surfaces, it is best to call upon professional help; we strongly advise against pouring concrete if there's a chance that temperatures will fall to the freezing point or under. If there is a risk of overnight frost, place a plastic tarpaulin over the fresh concrete, then cover it with a layer of soil or sand and wait until the frost is over before removing the protection.

It is essential for the concrete to dry slowly, otherwise it can crack. This risk is all the greater when it covers a large surface.

During hot weather, in order to minimize evaporation, fresh concrete should also be covered with a plastic sheet, held in place by weights. This should be left on for about three days.

1 and 2 The roof terrace is an additional space for pleasure and doing nothing, where people can relax in complete privacy.
3 Natural or tinted lime gives the walls their velvety aspect.

TENTS

To filter the light and cover a space that has no roof, you may want to create a tent with a rough cotton sheet (with double hem) with eyelets on the ends (a shoemaker can add these), which you can hang with stainless steel cable (three mm) fixed to the wall with hooks. The use of stretching screws will allow you to vary the tautness. If the base is concrete, use a few steel pegs; for a hollow base (cinder bock or brick), use a suitable chemical sealant (Do-it-yourself stores). If the tent is in the form of a canopy, make sure there are eyelets in the center to facilitate the runoff of rainwater and to avoid pools of water accumulating. Tents that are easy to mount are available from large stores carrying decorative items or outdoor supplies.

Various types of concrete finishes are available. To avoid unsightly streaks left by tamping down the concrete with a wooden float, go over it a second time, smoothing the substance perpendicular to the direction of the first pass. For a very smooth surface, use a steel finishing float (available in all hardware and Do-it-yourself stores). For a coarser surface, you can use a soft brush or broom.

A successful terrace is one that is waterproof, so make sure you add a good coating to the floor and an effective drainage system for rainwater. Chose tough materials that are frostproof and skidproof. These qualities are generally mentioned on the packaging and in specialized catalogs.

Another concern: protection against the wind and any houses with a view onto the terrace. In both cases a low wall, trellis or pergola with creeping plants and annuals can do the trick. You can also buy ingenious teak palisades that do double duty as flower boxes. They shelter you from drafts and from prying eyes and can accommodate plants in square or round flowerpots. Finally, for a roof terrace to be accessible and safe, it should be surrounded by a safety fence at least one meter high. Adding a shed or greenhouse may require a building permit, as it could be considered an extension.

1 A successful roof terrace should be waterproof, protected from the wind and from indiscreet eyes.
2 Tiles and ceramic pieces randomly assembled can be used to create a patchwork floor with a most delightful effect.

PLANTS

To take advantage of the terrace in all seasons, focus on annuals and perennial plants. Don't forget the cascading varieties, which can fill in the space between the various materials and vegetation. Although trees with large roots may be impressive, they are not well suited to this setting. Opt for climbing bushes up to two meters in height (available in nurseries).

Plants and flowers on the terrace and patio have only very shallow soil at their disposal, and require particular care. Mulching the soil with straw, pine bark, or clay ball helps limit evaporation, which is always more rapid on terraces.

With an external tap, it is easy to water your pots by a drip system that is normally reserved for the garden. If there are numerous pots, a distribution in the shape of a T is the most logical approach. A main hose can be extended by smaller branches, ending in sprinklers. These systems have the advantage of being reusable for several years (garden centers).

1 A successful roof terrace should be waterproof, protected from the wind and from indiscreet eyes.
2 Tiles and ceramic pieces randomly assembled can be used to create a patchwork floor with a most delightful effect.

3

LIGHTING

Even if you put off installing lighting on the terrace until later, don't forget to install the electrical wiring at the time of construction. To save time and money (and avoid having to break walls later), it is best to design the terrace entirely before you begin building or renovation.

To brighten up your evenings, you can hang garlands of exterior lights from the trees (Habitat, Fly, Ikea), hang a star-studded canvas on a branch or screen, or run a string of lights through your bushes. For a refined decor, alternate various types of lighting: multicolored paper lanterns, storm lanterns, candles, torches, and garlands.

Scatter various light sources along the low walls and staircase: plant a handful of long, thin candles in small galvanized steel buckets filled with sand, to form lovely sparkling bouquets.

3 The plants on the terrace have limited soil and thus require particular care.

4 In the evening, to create a refined atmosphere on a roof terrace, it is a good idea to multiply the sources of light: lanterns, candles, torches, storm lanterns, etc.

4

Address Book

AUSTRALIA AND NEW ZEALAND

Leaf and Stone Garden Gallery
Garden Art Gallery at
The Geelong Wintergarden
– North African-style handmade tiles, fountains
| 51 McKillop Street | Geelong
| Australia
| Tel.: +61 35 22 18 083
| www.leafandstone.com.au

Fun Gifts
– Tagines, Moroccan teapots and glasses
| PO Box 2399 | Richmond South
| Victoria 3121 | Australia
| Tel.: +61 39 42 71 110
| www.fungifts.com.au

Ottoman Classics
– Garden and courtyard features, kitchen and bathroom panels, borders, tables, mosaics suitable for both interior and exterior use, with floral or Islamic geometric designs.
| 155 Sydney Road | Brunswick,
| Victoria 3056 | Australia
| Tel.: +61 39 38 12 235
| www.ottomanclassics.com

Out of Casablanca Pty Ltd
– Specializes in the importation of unique handmade decorations and furnishings that reflect the rare heritage of Moroccan craftsmanship. An exclusive range of indoor/outdoor furniture, ceramics, lanterns, rugs and carpets, pottery, ironwork, leathercrafts, brass and tiled tables, etc.
| 3 Koonya Circuit | Caringbah NSW 2229
| Australia
| Tel.: +61 29 52 56 554
| www.outofcasablanca.com.au

Building materials

Strawbale Construction
– Specializes in the supply and application of the following natural paints, renders and various surface treatment products.
| Tel./Fax: +61 24 44 35 282
| www.strawtec.com.au

Interplast [NZ] Ltd
Mr. Bernard Willems
– Dealers for Tierrafino Stone, which provides products for producing a *tadelakt* finish and other limewashes.
| P.O. Box 302-165 N.H.P.C
| Auckland | New Zealand
| Tel.: +64 94 15 55 33
| Email: interplast@xtra.co.nz

GIBRALTAR

Jana Moroccan Arts and Crafts
| Unit 6F | Casement Arcade
| Gibraltar
| Tel.: +35 04 28 24

IRELAND

Natural Surfaces

– A niche market tile company, specializing in marble, limestone, travertine, granite, terra-cotta, slate, porcelain, and handmade ceramic tiles. The business has been in existence for over fourteen years importing and distributing tiles.
| 66 Carrigmore Crescent, CityWest
| Co. Dublin, Ireland
| Tel.: +35 31 28 56 810
| www.natural-surfaces.com

The Moroccan Furnishing Company
– Warehouse in Dublin open by appointment. Fountains, rugs, furniture, objets d'art, wrought iron, handcrafted tiles and zellige, items in Thuya wood, lanterns, henna lamps.
| Tel.: +35 31-86 41 553
| www.mfc.ie

Stoneware Studios
– Dealer for Tierrafino Stone, manufacturers of a product called Tierrafino Stone Tadelakt Original, which can be used wherever tadelakt finishes are desired.
| Mr Hugh Dorrian
| Pillmore Youghal, Co. Cork
| Ireland
| Tel.: +35 32 49 01 17
| www.stonewarestudios.com

SINGAPORE

Arab Street
– Various Middle Eastern and Moroccan craft and gift shops, fabrics, baskets, etc.
| Kampong Gelam | Singapore

UNITED KINGDOM

Crabtree & Evelyn
– Carries a Moroccan line of fragrance, Nadira, in essential oil, room spray, candles. Various stores throughout the UK; see website for locations.
| www.crabtree-evelyn.co.uk

Dar Interiors
– Specializes in the design, import and supply of high quality handmade Moroccan products. Product range includes Moroccan tiles, zellige, painted wood furniture, tables, lighting, moucharaby, fireplaces, lanterns,

antiques, and decorative accessories all of which are individually handcrafted by highly skilled Moroccan craftsmen. Also provides advice on design to hotels, restaurants, residential settings in Moroccan style.
| Arch 11, Miles Street
| Vauxhall, London SW8 1RZ | UK
| Tel.: +44 20 77 20 96 78
| www.darinteriors.com

Designers Guild
– Fabrics include a Moroccan pattern "Alhambra" available in cushions, drapery.
| 277 Kings Road | London SW3 5EN
| UK
| Tel.: +44 20 78 93 74 00

Dibor
H. Walker House
– Cutlery, includes a Moroccan-style pattern called Marrakesh.
| Calder Road, Dewsbury
| West Yorkshire WF13 3JS | UK
| Tel.: +44 87 00 13 36 66
| www.dibor.co.uk

El Kenz
– Rubs, soft furnishings, lanterns, jewelry
| Shop 19 | Bourbon Hanby Antique
| Arcade | 151 Sydney Street, Chelsea
| London SW3 6NT | UK
| Tel. : +44 20 73 51 28 59

Fes
– Mosaic fountains, antique plates, and bowls
| High Street | Wimbledon Village
| London SW19 | UK
| Tel.: +44 20 89 44 13 84

Fez Omar Traditional Moroccan Goods
– Bazaar-style items: painted and carved wood furniture, lanterns, teapots
| 71 Golborne Road | London W10 5NP
| UK
| Tel.: +44 20 89 64 55 73
| www.shop-fez.co.uk

Frontiers
– Jewellry, old Moroccan amber and silver beads
| 37-39 Pembridge Road | London W11
| UK
| Tel.: +44 20 77 27 61 32

Habibi-Interiors
– Tiles, other items for home decor (brass and mosaic washbasins, brass lamps and lanterns, carved wooden chests, doors, shelves, windows. Also rents items for Moroccan themed parties, films or weddings.
| 1c, Greyhound Rd (off Harrow Road)
| London NW10 5QH | UK
| Tel.: +44 20 89 60 92 03
| www.habibi-interiors.com

Ikea
– For local stores throughout the United Kingdom see the website. Carries lanterns and other home furnishings.
| www.ikea.com/ms/en_GB/

Kasbah International Bazaar
| 93 Portobello Road
| London W11 2QB | UK
| Tel./Fax : +44 20 73 43 25 83
| www.kasbahonline.com

Larusi
– Located in Gospel Oak, North London and open by appointment. Specializes in imported Moroccan fabrics, especially weavings by the Berber tribes, including carpets and other home furnishings.
| 12 Vicars Road | London NW5 4NL
| UK
| Tel.: +44 20-74 28 02 56
| www.larusi.com

Liberty of London
– Brass lanterns, rugs, poufs, cushions and other Moroccan fabrics and some antique pieces, all handmade in Morocco.
| Regent Street | London W1B 5AH
| UK
| Tel.: +44 20 77 34 12 34
| www.liberty.co.uk

Madina
– Moroccan arts and handicrafts
| 58A Crofton Road, Camberwell
| London SE5 8NB | UK
| Tel.: +44 20 77 01 40 72
| Lagzouli@btinternet.com

Maison du Monde
Customer Service and Main Showroom (Acton)
| 273-279 The High Street, Acton
| London W3 9BT | UK
| Showroom Tel.: +44 20 89 93 55 59
| www.maisondumonde.com

Maroc Decor
– Moroccan rugs and carpets. By appointment only.
| Dartmouth House
| Dartmouth Place, Chiswick
| London W4 2RH | UK
| Tel.: +44 20 89 89 51 937
| www.marocdecor.com

Momo Restaurant, Tearoom and Bazaar
– Moroccan tearoom carries various craft items for sale: lanterns, teapots, glasses, trays, etc.
| 23-25 Heddon Street | London W1
| UK
| Tel.: +44 20 7434 4040
| www.momoresto.com

Moroccan Bazaar
– Established in 1970, this shop sells by mail order and from its cash and carry warehouse; specializes in sourcing unique artefacts that reflect the true heritage of Morocco. It offers rare pieces from cities across Morocco, and provides interior design consultation as well as organizing Moroccan themed events and catering.
| Unit 10, Cumberland Business Park
| 17 Cumber land Avenue, Park Royal
| London NW10 7RT | UK
| Tel.: +44 20 89 61 75 91
| www.moroccanbazaar.co.uk

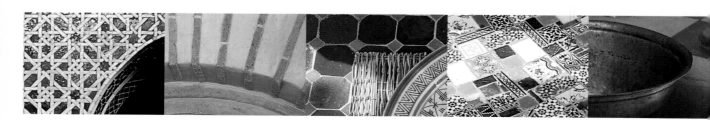

Morocco Elemental,
– Moorish mosaic furniture, fountains and candle lanterns.
| 67 Brushfield Street
| London E1 | UK
| Tel.: +44 20 72 47 75 88

The Pier (Retail) Ltd
– Stores all over Britain. See website for locations. They carry some Moroccan style items, such as mirrors, cushions, tables, chests.
| 9-12 North Central 127 | Milton Park
| Abingdon | OX14 4SA | UK
| Tel.: +44 84 56 09 11 234
| www.pier.co.uk

Rezai Carpets
– Carries good selection of antique and decorative carpets, rugs, kilims and cushions from the East and North Africa.
| 122 Portobello Road
| London W11 2ED | UK
| www.rezaipersiancarpets.com

Rhona Valentine Antique and Decorative Textiles, Islamic Art
– Islamic textiles, cushions, curtains, cottons, rugs, hangings.
| Antiquarius Antiques Centre K1-6
| 131-141 Kings Road
| London SW3 4PW | UK
| Tel..: +44 13 72 72 69 31
| www.rhonavalentine.co.uk

Spitalfields Market
– A stand selling contemporary Moroccan textiles, slippers, decorative objects, open Sundays in covered market.
| Commercial Street | London E1 | UK
| Tel.: +44 20 72 47 65 90

Talisman Trading Company
– Importers and wholesale suppliers of Moroccan handicrafts based, in part, on the natural resources of Morocco; they source rare and unusual pieces, tribal collections, objets d'art and also undertake international commercial and corporate commissions.
| Studio 2.05 | The Perfume Factory
| 140 Wales Farm Road
| London W3 6UG | UK
| Tel.: +44 20 88 96 17 17
| www.talisman-trading.co.uk/talisman.html

Tashi Limited
– Soft furnishings in natural fabrics.
| 118 Kensington Park Road
| London W11 2PW | UK
| Tel.: +44 20 77 27 17 57
| 82A Portobello Road
| London W11 ZQD | UK
| Tel.: +44 20 72 21 71 77
| www.tashi.co.uk

The Bride—Swiss Textiles
– Moroccan fashions, clothing, lanterns, teapots, painted wood items.
| 137 Edgware Road | London W2 2HR
| UK
| Tel.: +44 20 77 06 73 78
| Fax: +44 20 72 62 21 40

Zagora Interiors
– Moroccan crafts, lanterns, clothing, cushions, furniture, poufs, tables, fountains.
| 10-12 Fulham High Street
| London SW6 3LQ | UK
| Tel./Fax: +44 20 73 71 87 77
| www.zagorainteriors.com

OUTSIDE LONDON

Gallery Buzkashi
– Gallery specializing in Moroccan crafts, kilim-covered furniture, ceramics, gifts.
| 86A South Street
| Dorking, Surrey RH4 QEW | UK
| Tel.: +44 13 06 88 88 19

Maroc Design
| 397 Hanworth Road
| Hounslow TW4 5LF | UK
| Tel./Fax: +44 20 85 70 52 60
| Nezha30@hotmail.com

Gifts of Morocco
– Moroccan design crafts.
| 6 Open Market
| Francis Street Entrance, off London Road
| Brighton BN1 4JS | UK
| Tel.: +44 12 73 62 31 76

Casablanca Bazaar
– Tables, cushions, leather poufs, lamps, tables, candlesticks and mirrors, North African drums, Moroccan pipes and slippers, perfume bottles, wooden jewellery boxes, and jewellery.
| Arch U, Granary Wharf | Canal Basin
| Leeds LS1 4BR | UK
| Te.l: +44 11 32 45 55 77
| www.casablancabazaar.com

Kashef
– Ceramics, pottery and furniture
| 18 Salisbury Road
| Chorlton, Manchester M21 0SL
| United Kingdom
| Tel./Fax: +44 16 16 10 38 00

Casablanca
| 126a Harrogate Road
| Chapel Allerton, West Yorkshire LS7
4NZ | United Kingdom
| Tel.: +44 113 266 7790

Atlas Design (Northern) Ltd
– Wholesale and retail importer of Moroccan crafts, furniture and accessories for home and garden, purchases itsmerchandise on a fair trade basis from Moroccan artisans. Specializes in design requirements for restaurants, hotels, clubs and Moroccan theme events.
| Unit 10 Bridgewater Road
| Hertburn Industrial Estate
| Washington, Tyne and Wear NE37 2SG
| United Kingdom
| Tel.: +44 19 14 15 48 75
| www.atlasdesignuk.com/trade.asp

Kazzbar—The Moroccan Experience
– Importers of Moroccan furniture and design-led accessories for both indoors & out: wrought iron tables and chairs, terra-cotta garden pots, copper basins & mosaic fountains; for indoors ceramics from Safi, wrought iron screens, pouffes, henne candles, Moroccan kilims and rugs, leather slippers and shoes, lanterns, teapots, glasses and more.
| Unit 3a | Hamlyn House | Mardle Way
| Buckfastleigh | Devon TQ11 0NS | UK
| Tel.: +44 (08 00) 28 88 624 (freephone)
| Tel.: +44 77 33 07 05 77
| www.kazzbar.co.uk

Marrakech Design
– Furniture
| 4 London Street (Top of Walcott)
| Bath BA1 5BU | UK
| Tel.: +44 12 25 31 23 45
| max@morocco-travel.com

Soukous
– Moroccan ceramics, drums and textiles.
| 1a Pitville Place
| Cotham Hill, Bristol | UK
| Tel.: +44 11 79 23 98 54

Maison du Monde Furniture Clearance
| Warehouse (Croydon)
| Unit 1B, 500 Purley Way
| Croydon CR0 4RG | UK
| Tel.: +44 20 86 80 00 49

Online or catalog only

Global Treasures
– Furniture, marquetry, tables, sculptures, pots, bowls, trays.
| Tel./Fax: +44 17 43 24 20 92
| www.globaltreasures.biz

Maroque
– Internet only supplier, based in UK, sells by mail order around the world.
| Tel.: (0 14 49) 72 31 33 **24 hours a day**
| www.maroque.co.uk/faq.asp

Medina Online
– Online retail store specializing in Moroccan crafts, furniture.
| Tel.: +44 12 06 85 34 81
| www.medina-online.co.uk/

Momo Interiors
– Traditional and contemporary moroccan interiors, kitchenware, lighting, furniture, accessories.
| 34-35 The Colonnade | Piece Hall
| Halifax HX1 1RE | UK
| Order hotline
  Tel.: +44 87 03 00 20 74
| www.momo-interiors.com

Morocco Shop, Marrakesh
| www.morocco-shop.com/index.php

Moroccan Decor
– Sells via the internet but has a small storage unit where items can be viewed on appointment.
| Hemel Hempstead, Hertfordshire | UK
| Tel.: +44 20 89 52 71 37
| www.moroccandecor.co.uk

Building materials

B&Q
– Stores throughout the UK ; see website for local addresses. DIY store for paints, finishes, supplies for the patio or terrace.
| www.diy.com

Mike Wye and Associates
– Suppliers of natural building and decorating products, such as limewashes.
| Buckland Filleigh Sawmills
| Buckland Filleigh, Devon EX21 5RN
| UK | Tel.: +44 14 09 28 16 44
| www.mikewye.co.uk

Fired Earth Tiles
– Stores around the country; for locations see website. Moroccan flooring, design service, do home installations.
| Head Office
| 3 Twyford Mill, Oxford Road
| Adderbury, Nr Banbury, Oxfordshire
| OX17 3SX | UK
| Tel.: +44 84 53 66 04 00
| www.firedearth.com

Terra Firma tiles
– Carry Moroccan floor tiles, wall times, borders, mosaics, preassembled tiles.
| High Street | Stockbridge S020 5HF
| UK | Tel.: +44 12 64 81 03 15
| www.terrafirmatiles.co.uk

Johnstone's Paints
– See website for local distributors throughout Britain. They provide a service for previewing your colors and projects.
| Kalon Limited | Huddersfield Road
| Birstall, Batley
| West Yorkshire, WF17 9XA | UK
| Tel : +44 19 24 35 40 00
| www.johnstones-paints.co.uk

Construction Resources
– Britain's first ecological builders' merchant, and a center for ecological building, bringing together under one roof in central London a unique range of state-of-the-art building products and systems. Open to builders and the general public, their showroom or mail order service provides paints and finishes, including Tierrafino Stone products for producing a tadelakt finish for bathroom, sauna, and hammam walls. They also have seminars and technical documentation on doing it yourself.
| 16 Great Guilford Street
| London SE1 0HS | UK
| Tel.: +44 20 74 50 22 11
| www.constructionresources.com

MOROCCO

Boudlal Afif
– High quality goatskin henna lamps in large choice of motifs, mail order available.
| 12 rue de la Skala
| Essaouira
| Tel.: + 212 44 47 64 29

Akkal
– Moroccan dinnerware in terra-cotta with a contemporary appearance.
| Quartier industriel Sidi Ghanem
| 322, Marrakesh
| Tel.: +212 44 33 59 38

Ahmed Laghrissi
– Producer of fine traditional dinnerware in very small quantities.
| 9 souk des Potiers, Safi
| Tel.: +212 66 12 21 62

BOOKS

Jean-Marc Castera, ARABESQUES: DECORATIVE ART IN MOROCCO, trans. Kirk McElhearn.
Paris: ACR Edition Internationale Courbevoie, 1999.

James F. Jereb, ARTS AND CRAFTS OF MOROCCO. London: Thames and Hudson, 1995.

D. and L. Landt, LIVING IN MOROCCO: DESIGN FROM CASABLANCA TO MARRAKESH.
London: Thames and Hudson, 1995.

Mary Schoeser, WORLD TEXTILES: A CONCISE HISTORY. London: Thames and Hudson, 2003.

Philippa Scott, TURKISH DELIGHTS. London: Thames and Hudson, 2001.

Lisa Lovatt-Smith, MOROCCAN INTERIORS/INTERIEURS MAROCAINS. Cologne: Taschen, 2004

Barbara and René Stoeltie, LIVING IN MOROCCO. Cologne: Taschen, 2001; Thames and Hudson, 2003.

Susan Sully and Jean Cazals, THE NEW MOROCCAN STYLE: THE ART OF SENSUAL LIVING.
New York: Carlson Potter, 2003; London: Thames and Hudson, 2005.

Corinne Verner, Cecile Tréal, Jean-Michel Ruiz, VILLAS AND RIADS OF MOROCCO,
New York. Harry N. Abrams, 2005

Herbert Ypma, MOROCCO MODERN. New York: Stewart, Tabori and Chang, 1996.

ACKNOWLEDGMENTS

Guest houses and *riads*

HOTEL VILLA MAROC, 10, rue 1. Ben Yassine, Essaouira. Tel.: + 212 44 47 61 47

DAR BAOUSSALA, Douar El Ghazoua, Essaouira. Tel.: + 212 44 47 53 46

DAR LOULEMA, 2, rue Souss, Essaouira. Tel.: + 212 44 55 74 06 86

LA MAISON BLEUE, 2, place de l'Istiqlal–Batha, Fez. Tel.: + 212 55 74 06 86

MARRAKECH MEDINA. Tel.: + 212 44 44 24 28

RIAD ENJIA, Dherb Mes Fioui,9, Marrakesh. Tel.: + 212 44 44 09 26

Architects

ELIE MOUYAL / Marrakesh, Tel.: + 212 4 30 05 02.

CHARLES BOCCRA / Marrakesh, Tel.: + 212 4 43 00 30. Fax: + 212 4 43 60 66